Being Tommy Cooper

Tom Green

A SAMUEL FRENCH ACTING EDITION

SAMUELFRENCH.COM
SAMUELFRENCH-LONDON.CO.UK

FOR PRODUCTION ENQUIRIES

UNITED STATES AND CANADA
Info@SamuelFrench.com
1-866-598-8449

UNITED KINGDOM AND EUROPE
Plays@SamuelFrench-London.co.uk
020-7255-4302

Each title is subject to availability from Samuel French, depending upon country of performance. Please be aware that BEING TOMMY COOPER may not be licensed by Samuel French in your territory. Professional and amateur producers should contact the nearest Samuel French office or licensing partner to verify availability.

MUSIC USE NOTE

IMPORTANT BILLING AND CREDIT REQUIREMENTS

TOMMY COOPER MATERIAL

BEING TOMMY COOPER was first produced by Old Bomb Theatre at the Old Red Lion Theatre, London, on 12th June 2012. The performance was directed by Cecily Boys and designed by Zahra Mansouri, with lighting design by Simeon Miller and sound design by Max Pappenheim. The cast was as follows:

TOMMY COOPER	Damian Williams
MIFF FERRIE	James Benson
BILLY GLASON	Gerald McDermott

This version of the play was first produced by Franklin Productions at the Yvonne Arnaud Theatre, Guildford, on 3rd May 2013 as part of a UK tour. The performance was directed by Cecily Boys and designed by Susannah Henry, with lighting design by Simeon Miller and sound design by Max Pappenheim. The cast was as follows:

TOMMY COOPER	Damian Williams
MIFF FERRIE	Halcro Johnston
BILLY GLASON	Morgan Deare
MARY KAY	Rebecca Thorn

CHARACTERS

BILLY GLASON
MIFF FERRIE
TOMMY COOPER
MARY KAY

SCENE

The action throughout takes place on a split stage:

i) <u>March 1954:</u> A small dressing room in which Tommy Cooper is getting dressed ready to go on stage. This could double as the hotel room.

ii) <u>March 1954</u>: The floor of a Las Vegas hotel casino. Late at night (not that you'd know; this place looks the same whether it's 3am or 3pm)

iii) <u>1969</u>: A small room backstage at a large theatre – perhaps even a caretaker's cupboard. A table almost fills the space, with a phone, a typewriter and a pile of paper and notebooks.

iv) There will also need to be a performance area for Tommy Cooper – plus space later for The Windermere Club, a restaurant table and for Mary's scene.

A NOTE ON COOPER'S MAGIC

It should be possible to master the tricks included as part of Cooper's performance without prior experience. Some tricks do require special props: notably the metal rings, the "bottle and glass" and the dipping duck. These are widely available and come with instructions. The egg drop trick simply requires a plastic tray, egg cups (or similar) and fake eggs (just in case it goes wrong!) Done correctly the trick looks impressive but, in fact, is just a version of "pulling the tablecloth" – ie. the eggs, or some of them, will drop into the cups when the tray is knocked away at speed. Free videos explaining how to master all of the tricks are widely available on the internet.

Tom Green

ACT ONE

Casino Floor – 1954

(**BILLY GLASON**, *a 50-year-old Jewish Bostonian, is perched on a bar stool staring into a glass from which he never drinks. He looks dishevelled and depressed and is fiddling with a single dollar on the table.*)

Backstage Room – 1969

(**MIFF FERRIE**, *a smartly-dressed Scot in his fifties, is sitting at the table, taking a phone call.*)

Casino Floor – 1954

(*It becomes apparent that* **GLASON** *is keeping half an eye on a slot machine across the room. He glances at his watch.*)

GLASON. I should just go to bed. You can't change a bad day into a good day after one a.m. That's a fact of life.

(*He notices someone approaching the slot machine.*)

But... We're back in play. We're back in play. (*He continues watching and perhaps mimes pulling the arm of the slot machine.*) One...nothing. Two...nothing. Three...a dollar; a lonely rattle. Four...sounds like three dollars won. And they are going straight back in. Nothing. Nothing. Nothing. One more? He's searching in his pants for one last dollar. There it is, and…nothing. Ouch. *(He watches the man walk away and then looks at the dollar in his own hand.)*

Dressing Room

*(***TOMMY COOPER*** *comes into the dressing room wearing casual clothes, holding a suit-bag and a fez-shaped hatbox. He sits down.)*

Casino Floor – 1954

GLASON. Have you ever been to Las Vegas? It's a dump. Seriously. Everything you've ever heard about it is true. All the bad things. You can see straight away why they tested atom bombs here. Some nights I go to bed praying they'll set off another one while I'm asleep. There's not much anyone would miss.

(Noticing more action near the slot machine)

Hello…? No, she's just browsing.

Sure, there's a lot of building going on but that just makes it worse. People say in five years time it will be spectacular but I don't care about five years time, I care about here and now. I probably won't even be alive in 1959. And I hate this place. The desert. The noise. The people. It's a goddamn hell-hole. Especially when you've had the kind of night I've had.

Hotel Room – 1954

*(After collecting his thoughts for a moment, ***COOPER*** pours himself a drink and downs it. He pours himself another, and leaves it for a moment.)*

Casino Floor – 1954

GLASON. *(looking across)* She's back! She browsed and now she's back. Studying the payout. Looking in her purse. Come on, lady, just play. Maybe you'll get lucky. Maybe it will be you.

I've been watching this machine for an hour and a half. Ever since I came down from a meeting with a guy here. A comedian. Tommy Cooper. To whom I was hoping to make a sale. But to whom no goddamn sale was made.

Fifteen people have played it and it's only paid out about seventy per cent. Which is low. They sometimes pay out over ninety per cent of what gets put in – you know, to keep you coming back.

I should just go to bed. But it's only paid out seventy per cent for an hour and a half and not once has it coughed up a jackpot. Not once have the three bars lined up.

Dressing Room

*(**COOPER** downs the second drink and then starts to get undressed. He looks weary.)*

Backstage Room – 1969

*(**MIFF FERRIE** is wrapping up the phone call.)*

FERRIE. Uh-huh.

Like I said, I'll see what I can do.

1970 is going to be a very busy year for us.

I have to go.

I have to—

There's a call on the other line. *(He makes the phone briefly engaged – there is no other line.)*

I'll call you back just as soon as I know anything definite. Goodnight.

(He puts the phone down, and makes very neat notes about the call in his notebook. He continues doing this while he talks to the audience.)

Everyone thinks their own time is the most valuable, don't they? Christ! But the truth is that they need us more than we need them. You have to believe that.

Dressing Room

*(**COOPER** stands in his underwear – perhaps looking at himself in the mirror, as if in a trance. He pours another drink. And leaves it a moment.)*

Backstage Room – 1969

FERRIE. I should make them come to me. Forget about business on the phone. Keep them waiting outside with lukewarm coffee for half an hour and make them beg us to play their shabby little theatre.

Not here, of course. I have a proper office. But when Tommy's got a long-running show I like to carve out a place for myself. Backstage. It's not always easy getting a phone line in but it means I can keep track of him. I can see what else is going on, hear the gossip. Feel the atmosphere.

I like it.

Casino Floor – 1954

GLASON. *(looking across)* Finally. A dollar in, and…clunk, clunk, clunk! Five bucks back. Nice start. What? You're walking away?! *(Laughs)* You win five dollars and walk away?! I take my hat off to you, lady.

Most people in her position, 99.9% of people here, gamblers, would pile that money straight back into the slot because you win five bucks on your first pull and you obviously feel good. About yourself. About the machine. And suddenly you're rich. You've got five shiny silver dollars burning a hole in your hand so it's only natural to pop one in, and then another and another…

(Looks at his watch) I should just go to bed.

Dressing Room

(**COOPER** *downs the drink. And gets dressed in his tuxedo.*)

Backstage Room – 1969

FERRIE. I used to work on the other side of the curtain, of course. Did you know that? A million years ago. Well, before the war mostly – 30 years ago. And I suppose that's another reason why I feel happy back here. But, you know, I've come to realise that this is more challenging and more creative. Being an agent. Managing talent. Think about it, there are a lot of great acts out there but only a handful of great agents. What does that tell you?

(Blackout)

Onstage

(Note: canned laughter should be used throughout this scene.)

(**TOMMY COOPER** *takes the stage holding a red silk cloth.*)

COOPER. Thank you. Thank you very much.

(Laughs)

Thank you. Good evening.

(To offstage) Have I got time for more?

(He continues.) I shall now produce from this empty cloth, four live ducks.

(He opens the cloth to reveal that a large hole is cut in the middle.) They got away again.

(He discards the cloth, paces the stage.)

Look. *(Standing on one leg, he flexes the knee of the loose leg.)* See that? This one does the same. *(He repeats with the other leg.)*

(laughs)

Here's a little trick I'd like to show you now. It's the very famous ping pong ball and handkerchief trick. Easy for me to say.

(He takes a ping pong ball and a handkerchief.) Here's the ping pong ball, here's the hankie. *(Sneezes, blows his nose on the handkerchief and then discards it. Digs in pockets and finds a paper bag.)*

As I was saying. This is the very famous ping pong ball and paper bag trick. *(Laughs. Sneezes. Blows nose on paper bag and then discards it. Digs in pockets and finds a rubber chicken.)*

Ladies and gentlemen, the very famous ping pong ball and rubber chicken trick! *(To offstage)* What the…?! *(Sneezes. Starts to blow his nose on the rubber chicken, but then discards it. Laughs. Finds another handkerchief in his pocket.)*

Ping pong ball, hankie. Hankie, ping pong ball.

(Breaks off, scratches his teeth.)

My teeth itch. I went to the dentist and he said my teeth are all right but my gums have got to come out. And I said… *(laughs)* He looked at me and I said, 'I've got a terrible pain just up there' *(indicates cheek)* You see. Up there it was. So he said, 'I'll tell you what I'll do' and I said 'What's that?' Because he spoke to me. And I said 'I've got a pain up there.' And he said 'I'll tell you what, I'll x-ray it.' So he got these little tiny x-rays like that *(indicates)* – little small ones like that. And he put it up there like that. *(Holds lip up over tooth with a finger)* And I'm sitting there like that and he brings this x-ray machine in, see. Right there. And it went z-z-z. Just like that. And he took it out and he looked at it and he said, 'No wonder it hurts, you've got a finger poking up there.'

(Laughs)

(Holds up the ball and hankie in turn)

Ball, hankie. Hankie, ball.

(Breaks off, laughs)

You know, that dentist, the same dentist, asked me to tell him a joke. Tell me a joke, he said. *(Shrugs)* So I thought for a bit, I thought, I did, and I was lying there, just like this – my head back like that – *(laughs)* and I thought, he's got a drill, I'd better make it a good one. So I thought, I did, and *(laughs)* I said *(holds mouth wide open so that words can't be understood as he speaks)*

(Laughs; indicates for the audience to laugh more)

(Holds up ball)

Before your very eyes this ping pong ball will disappear completely. *(To offstage)* Will it? *(Laughs)*

(Breaks off)

Ooh my feet are killing me. You know, every night when I'm in bed they get me round the throat like that trying to strangle me.

(Brandishes ball)

Now I want you to watch me very, very closely. And if you see any suspicious movements don't say anything. Before your very eyes this ball will disappear completely. No ping. No pong. No ball. *(Turns offstage)* Are you sure?

(He puts the ball in the bag.)

On the other hand... *(Looks at his other hand)* I've got four fingers and a thumb.

(One hand is now in the bag.)

(Laughs)

Oh dear.

(He crumples the bag with the other hand and then very obviously whips the other hand out and appears to put the ball under his left arm. He looks at the audience with mock-innocence. He turns the bag inside out.)

Look – it's vanished right in front of your very eyes. You haven't the slightest clue where it's gone. Have you? Eh? Where? Under my arm?

(He lifts up the right arm.)

No. The other one?

(He turns his back to the audience and lifts up the right arm.)

(Turns back to face front)

This one? *(Indicating left arm)*

No. *(He lifts it very slightly, as if hiding the ball.)*

Higher? How's that? *(He raises the arm completely – the ball isn't there.)* Hah!

(Steps back, pleased with himself)

Thank you. Thank you very much.

(Breaks off)

You know, I had a meal last night. I had everything on the menu. They'd run out of plates. And I said to this waiter, I said, this chicken I've got here is cold. And he said, 'It should be, it's been dead two weeks.'

(Pause for laughter)

I said, 'Not only that,' I said. I said. I said it twice. I said, 'It's got one leg shorter than the other. He said, 'What do you want to do, eat it or dance with it?'

(Pause for laughter)

I said, 'Forget the chicken…'

(Laughs)

(Aside) It's making me giggle now.

I said, 'Forget the chicken…' *(Laughs)* I said, 'Give me a lobster.' So he brought the lobster. I looked at it and I said, 'Just a minute…' I said, 'Just a minute,' I said. I said, 'It's only got one claw.' He said, 'Well it's been in a fight.' I said, 'Well give me the winner.'

(Pause, and then laughs)

Hotel Room

(March 1954. Slightly earlier on the same night as in GLASON's casino scenes. A plain hotel room in Las Vegas.)

(TOMMY COOPER, *having got offstage an hour earlier, is sitting on the bed with a large brandy in one hand and the bottle in the other.)*

(BILLY GLASON *is standing facing him.)*

(On the bed next to **COOPER** *are two large hand-bound volumes.* **GLASON** *looks between* **COOPER** *and the books.)*

GLASON. Like I say, that's just a sample. I have twenty-four more volumes, just as big, ready and waiting.

COOPER. Did you see the show?

GLASON. Which show?

COOPER. Which show?!

GLASON. Sorry, I—

COOPER. *(interrupting)* Our show. My show. Tonight.

GLASON. No.

COOPER. You didn't see it?

GLASON. No. I was meant to come tonight but I got delayed.

COOPER. Doing what?

GLASON. I only just got into town. But I will come. It's top of my list. I saw the notices in *Variety*. That's why I wanted to meet with you.

COOPER. Variety hated it.

GLASON. But they liked you. 'Tommy Cooper proves to be the high spot of the show.'

COOPER. The high spot of something they hated.

GLASON. They didn't hate it.

COOPER. What did you think? Oh sorry, I forgot, you didn't come. You've come to my hotel room at, what, midnight…

GLASON. It's just gone eleven.

COOPER. …trying to flog me *Encyclopaedia Britannica* but you didn't actually see the show.

GLASON. It's not *Encyclopaedia Britannica*.

COOPER. They liked my prestidigitation.

GLASON. Who did?

COOPER. You said you'd read *Variety*.

GLASON. I don't remember…

COOPER. 'The unexpected climaxes to Cooper's tricks are smooth prestidigitations tailored to laughs.' No wonder no one's coming. Anyway, they're right.

GLASON. Who?

COOPER. *Variety.* The show's a mess. You know what they said about it? They said it moves 'heavily'. Christ. That's a damning word, isn't it. Or was it Vera Lynn? Did they say Vera Lynn moves heavily?

GLASON. I don't know.

COOPER. You know who she is?

GLASON. Vera Lynn? Of course.

COOPER. No one else seems to. You should have come to the show – she'd have enjoyed having at least one person left in the audience when she finished. *(Pause)* Go on then, make me laugh.

GLASON. Excuse me?

COOPER. Tell me a joke.

GLASON. I'm not here to tell—

COOPER. *(interrupting)* Tell me the best one from your books. Your compendiums.

GLASON. Well, it's all a matter of taste but if you look—

COOPER. *(interrupting)* I said tell me, don't show me. Have you started? Is this part of it?

GLASON. I don't want to pick out a single one. The whole idea is that the books provide a huge selection from which you can choose.

COOPER. Not funny.

GLASON. Pardon?

COOPER. I'm not laughing.

GLASON. I wasn't trying to make you laugh.

COOPER. That's a novel approach. I'm not sure it will catch on but I'll give you another chance. If you make me laugh I'll buy the whole damn lot. How many was it again?

GLASON. Twenty-six volumes. Three thousand dollars.

COOPER. That's funny. But not in a good way.

GLASON. Mr Cooper, I can tell jokes.

COOPER. Great.

GLASON. I grew up telling jokes.

COOPER. Tell me one now.

GLASON. But that's not what I'm here for.

(**COOPER** *lies down on the bed and closes his eyes.*)

GLASON. Goodnight, Mr Cooper. I'd like to say it's been a pleasure but it hasn't.

(**GLASON** *leaves. A few moments later he returns. As he does so,* **COOPER** *sits up and grabs the books.*)

I forgot…

(**COOPER** *guffaws.*)

COOPER. Brilliant. Brilliant! You storm out, but forget the books! You're killing me.

(*His laughter cuts out instantly. Businesslike, he starts to browse through the books.*)

So you're a writer?

GLASON. Not exactly.

COOPER. You didn't write these?

GLASON. I improved them.

COOPER. Debatable.

GLASON. Bob Hope doesn't think so.

COOPER. (*deadpan, reading*) 'He wasn't bald. His head just grew up through his hair.' 'She's always making mountains out of moth balls'. 'Every time he gets a raise she gets a new hat. Success is going to her head.' (*He blows imaginary dust off the pages.*) Dusty. (*Reads*) 'Marriage is a union that allows a man to work for a boss without pay'

GLASON. Just give them back.

COOPER. You do jokes for Bob Hope?

GLASON. I do.

COOPER. Everyone does jokes for Bob Hope.

GLASON. He has a copy of the collection. As does Steve Allen. And Jonny Carson. And Ed Sullivan.

COOPER. So you're trying to sell me gags that everyone else has already used.

GLASON. They are a select few.

COOPER. Selected how?

GLASON. They are—

COOPER. *(interrupting)* …prepared to pay three thousand dollars.

GLASON. Mr Cooper you've obviously had a hard day. So have I. You've obviously had a drink.

COOPER. Cheers.

GLASON. …but I am a professional. I came here this evening because I had heard about you and wanted to meet you and thought you might be interested in buying some of my wares. I am sorry that I wasn't able to get to your show. I look forward to coming tomorrow night. Let me start over. My name is Billy Glason. I was a singer and a comic on Vaudeville for many years. I played the Orpheum Circuit. I did okay. I wasn't a star but I did okay. You know? And somewhere along the line I started to note down some of the gags I kept hearing five times a day. And once I'd started I couldn't stop. And because I could, I tweaked them here and there. Updating them a little. Giving them a bit more rhythm. More punch. And I collected and collected until I had the twenty-six volumes I'm offering you tonight. An encyclopaedia of gags.

COOPER. Have you sold it to anyone else in Britain?

GLASON. No. There's only a handful in circulation over here. None over there.

COOPER. So I'll have exclusive use – in Britain.

GLASON. At the moment, yes.

COOPER. And for all time.

GLASON. I'd need to speak to my lawyer.

COOPER. It's a small country.

GLASON. We'll see.

COOPER. Thing is, I don't really do gags.

GLASON. What do you mean?

COOPER. Didn't anyone tell you? If you'd seen the show you'd have known. I'm a magician.

Backstage Room – 1969

(**FERRIE** *is on the phone.*)

FERRIE. *(answering the phone)* – Hello, Miff Ferrie speaking.
Hello? Is anyone there? Who is this?

Gwen?

What's wrong?

Okay, calm down.

I need you to calm down.

Just tell me what's happened. Is it Tommy? Has
something happened to—

What?!

(He listens.)

Is he there now? Gwen? Is Tommy there now?

Yes, I can hear them.

Is Tommy there with you?

Are you okay? I mean, are you hurt?

Right.

What would you like me to do?

Gwen, you don't mean that.

You don't mean that, Gwen.

You can't do that.

Is he there? Let me speak to him.

Gwen?

It will be all right. Let me speak to him and it will be
all right.

Let me speak to Tommy.

Gwen?

(She has put the phone down.)

Onstage

(Spotlight on **COOPER** *performing as before. Canned laughter, as before.)*

COOPER. I'd like to tell you… *(Laughs)* I'd like to tell you… *(Laughs)* I'd like to tell you a little bit about my childhood. I was born at a very early age; I cried like a baby. I was a surprise to my parents. They found me on the doorstep. They were expecting a bottle of milk.

(Paces)

Oh dear.

You know, I had my mother on the phone. I did. I said, *(laughs)* I'm about to do my show. She said, 'Are you having me on?' I said, I'll give you an audition but I'm not promising anything. *(Laughs)*

Backstage Room – 1969

*(***FERRIE*** sits for a moment and then picks up the phone and dials.)*

(There is no reply. He puts the phone down.)

FERRIE. The thing is, I'm his agent, not his bloody keeper. Why should I worry so that he can be carefree? Why should I be meticulous so that he can do whatever he likes?

Onstage

COOPER. *(laughs)* Good this, isn't it? That was a rhetorical question. You know what rhetorical means, don't you? Neither do I. *(Laughs)*

I was born in Wales… That wasn't a joke. *(Laughs)* I was born in Wales. And I always wanted to be a comedian. *(Laughs)* Still do!

Backstage Room – 1969

FERRIE. We've been together a long time. Me and Tommy. When I first met him he wasn't even funny.

The Windermere Club – 1947

(**MIFF FERRIE** *is sitting on a chair, smoking, and flicking through a selection of sheet music.* **TOMMY COOPER**, *clearly nervous, is standing on the 'stage' – waiting.*)

FERRIE. *(without looking up)* What's your range?

COOPER. Excuse me?

FERRIE. Your vocal range. I can hear that's a good strong baritone but I'd like to hear you do something a little more subtle.

COOPER. I'm not a—

FERRIE. *(holding out some sheet music)* Try this.

COOPER. I'm a—

FERRIE. *Galway Bay.* You won't know it. It's new. Just came in this week. You can sight read can't you?

COOPER. Sight read?

FERRIE. Music. And I like to hear people sing unaccompanied. That's not a problem is it? Or do you need a piano?

COOPER. No. I don't need a piano, Mr Ferrie.

FERRIE. Good.

COOPER. Because I'm not a singer.

FERRIE. What?

COOPER. I'm a… I do an act. I've got an act. That I do.

FERRIE. An act?

COOPER. Yes. Funny. Hopefully.

FERRIE. What did you say your name was?

COOPER. Cooper, sir. Tommy Cooper.

FERRIE. Ah.

COOPER. Hello.

FERRIE. And you're not a singer?

COOPER. No.

FERRIE. Are you sure?

COOPER. Yes.

FERRIE. Would you like to give it a go?

COOPER. Not really.

FERRIE. It's a lovely tune. *(Sings)*

"IF YOU EVER GO ACROSS THE SEA TO IRELAND,
THEN MAYBE, AT THE CLOSING OF YOUR DAY,
YOU CAN SIT AND WATCH THE MOON RISE OVER
    CLADDAGH
AND SEE THE SUN GO DOWN ON GALWAY BAY."

Not really my taste but we try to cater for all sorts here.

Is it 'Claddagh', or 'Claddagh', do you think?

COOPER. I don't know.

FERRIE. Pretty, though, isn't it?

(FERRIE looks back at the music.)

(And now when he sings, it is full-throated, as if in a large theatre.)

FERRIE. *(Sings)*

"JUST TO HEAR AGAIN THE RIPPLE OF THE TROUT STREAM,
THE WOMEN IN THE MEADOW MAKING HAY,
JUST TO SIT BESIDE A TURF FIRE IN THE CABIN
AND WATCH THE BAREFOOT GOSSOONS AT THEIR PLAY."

(On the final line his voice cracks out of tune, and he starts to cough.)

FERRIE. I'm out of practice.

COOPER. Would you like me to do it?

FERRIE. Do what?

COOPER. My act.

FERRIE. Someone told me you were a singer.

COOPER. I'm not.

(A silence. FERRIE is still browsing through the sheet music.)

FERRIE. Go on then.

COOPER. *(pause)* Hello, good evening and welcome to the show. *(To offstage)* Have I got time for more? *(Laughs)* I'd like to start with some impressions. First of all the inimitable James Cagney. 'You dirty rat. You dirty double crossin' rat.' *(Aside)* What does inimitable mean?

(Mimes hunchback, does Charles Laughton voice) 'I'm not a man...'

(Stands upright) I am. *(Laughs)* I am a man. This is just pretending.

(Mimes hunchback)

(Stands upright) Just in case you were wondering.

(Mimes hunchback)

(Stands upright) I said I was doing impressions. Pay attention. *(Laughs)*

(Mimes hunchback, Charles Laughton voice) 'I am not a man and I am not a beast.' *(Cries)*

(Stands upright. Laughs.) Good this, isn't it? Don't answer that. *(Laughs)*

'I am not a man and I am not a beast. *(Cries)* I am shapeless as the man in the moon.' *(Cries)*

(Stands upright) Whaddya mean who was it? *(To offstage)* Who was it? Oh yes. Quasi-what's it. The Hunchback Of... *(To offstage)* Golders Green? Notre Dame. *(Laughs)* Oh yes. The great Charles Laughton. *(Charles Laughton voice)* 'Why am I not made of stone like thee?!'

(Mimes hunchback, normal voice) Oops I forgot.

(Stands upright, Charles Laughton voice) 'Why am I not made of—'

(Mimes hunchback, normal voice) I forgot again.

(Stands upright, Charles Laughton voice) 'Why am I not—'

*(Seeing that **MIFF** is paying no attention. **COOPER** breaks off.)*

COOPER. Mr Ferrie?

FERRIE. What? Sorry? *(Looks at his watch)* Crikey, is that the time?

London Street – 1969

*(**MARY KAY** is waiting alone.)*

*(**COOPER** appears with an bag full of tricks and props.)*

MARY. Hello!

*(**COOPER** hands her two Chinese linking rings.)*

TOMMY. Hold these.

MARY. Have you been shopping again?

TOMMY. They're on loan.

MARY. Why did you want to meet so early?

TOMMY. Here.

(He passes her two more rings.)

MARY. Our train doesn't leave until this afternoon.

*(**COOPER** takes out a 'sword' and pretends to swallow it.)*

Do you want to get a room…?

*(**COOPER** 'swallows' the trick sword and beckons for applause.)*

MARY. *(cont.)* …on a Sunday?

*(**COOPER** takes the 'sword' out of his mouth and presses it closed, revealing the trick. He laughs.)*

COOPER. Watch this.

*(**COOPER** takes two of the four rings from **MARY** and clanks them together 'proving' them to be solid.)*

(He then links them just like that – and is delighted.)

(He then links all four.)

(He then makes to unlink them, but they remain stubbornly locked together. He coughs and looks apologetic. Laughs. Tries again. Nothing. He looks comically crestfallen, then throws them to the floor. And laughs.)

MARY. Brilliant.

*(**COOPER** has put on a fez with an arrow through it.)*

COOPER. I've got a splitting headache. *(Laughs)*

MARY. Come on, we can look at what you bought later.

COOPER. *(reading from a book)* I've always been unlucky. I had a rocking horse once, and it died. *(Laughs)*

MARY. We can make this a special day.

COOPER. I went to the doctor's the other day and I said, 'It hurts when I do that.' And he said, 'Don't do it then.'

(Both laugh)

*(**COOPER** hands her the bags.)*

COOPER. I'll see you later.

MARY. What do you mean?

COOPER. I've got a date, Mary.

MARY. Who with?

*(**COOPER** doesn't reply, and is already on his way.)*

MARY. *(calling after him)* I'll see you on the train.

Casino Floor – 1954

*(The hotel casino: **GLASON** is perched on the stool as before.)*

GLASON. How would you describe the smell of a Las Vegas casino? What can you smell? I always notice the disinfectant. The cleanest restrooms anywhere in America.

I'm a salesman myself, so I know the tricks. That's what I was doing earlier – trying to sell. So I know what this is all about – attention to detail, trying to make you feel special.

But the restrooms are too clean, you know. And that smell is too much. Overpowering. Nauseating.

(He looks at his watch.) I should go to bed.

Hotel Room – 1954

(The hotel room in Las Vegas, as before. Moments later.)

(There is a knock at the door and then, without waiting for an answer, **MIFF FERRIE** *comes in.)*

*(***FERRIE** *is surprised to see anyone there apart from* **COOPER**.*)*

FERRIE. Oh.

COOPER. Unbelievable!

FERRIE. I didn't know you had company.

COOPER. He knocks and then walks straight in!

FERRIE. *(to* **GLASON***)* Miff Ferrie.

GLASON. Billy Glason.

FERRIE. I hope I'm not interrupting.

COOPER. You are.

GLASON. I was just leaving.

COOPER. Billy's a salesman.

FERRIE. *(to* **GLASON***)* What do you sell?

COOPER. Encyclopaedias.

FERRIE. *(to* **GLASON***)* Oh. We're not resident here so I don't think we'll be needing a collection of—

COOPER. Not those kind of encyclopaedias. Gags.

FERRIE. *(to* **GLASON***)* You're a writer?

COOPER. Not exactly.

FERRIE. *(to* **GLASON***)* We always need writers.

COOPER. He's not a writer.

FERRIE. Well he doesn't say much.

> (**COOPER** *laughs.*)

GLASON. I'll leave my card.

COOPER. *(to* **FERRIE***)* How much do you think he wants for them?

FERRIE. For what?

COOPER. His jokes.

FERRIE. I've no idea.

COOPER. Twenty-six volumes the same as this. Thin paper. Closely typed. How much?

FERRIE. Too much. *(Sarcastic, at* **COOPER***'s expense)* Writers always want too much – don't they?

COOPER. Three thousand buckeroos.

GLASON. Ever write your own material?

COOPER. Does Picasso make his own paintbrushes?

FERRIE. *(to* **COOPER***)* We need to talk.

GLASON. *(to* **COOPER***)* How much are you willing to pay?

FERRIE. In private.

COOPER. *(to* **GLASON***)* How low are you prepared to go? *(To* **FERRIE***)* That sounds ominous.

> (**COOPER** *pours himself a large drink.*)

GLASON. I'll take two thousand five hundred dollars cash – if you pay this week.

FERRIE. Tommy…

COOPER. *(to* **GLASON***)* What about exclusivity?

GLASON. You can choose your favourite five hundred gags and I'll remove those from any future UK sales.

COOPER. And US sales as well – your lot are always coming over these days.

GLASON. *(pause)* It's a deal.

COOPER. And not five hundred gags. Fifteen hundred.

GLASON. What?

COOPER. And certainly not two and a half thousand dollars.

GLASON. Goodnight.

FERRIE. Goodnight, Mr…

COOPER. Glason.

(**GLASON** *reaches for the books but* **COOPER** *holds them out of reach and starts to read again.*)

FERRIE. Tommy, I have some news.

COOPER. 'My golf is improving. I'm missing the hole much closer than I used to.' (*To* FERRIE) What do you think?

FERRIE. Important news.

COOPER. (*to* GLASON) I don't know why I'm asking him.

FERRIE. The show's closing.

COOPER. He never thinks anything I do is funny.

(*A silence*)

FERRIE. They're closing the show. Goodnight, Mr Glason. We've got your card.

(**COOPER** *is still holding the books.*)

COOPER. He can stay.

FERRIE. He wants to leave.

COOPER. (*rapid*) No he doesn't. Do you? See.

FERRIE. There's a lot we need to talk about.

COOPER. (*rapid*) He won't tell anyone – you won't tell anyone will you? Have a drink. We're still negotiating. You're not rushing off anywhere are you? Cheers. To America! (*To* FERRIE) So how much will this cost me?

FERRIE. We can talk about it in the morning.

COOPER. When does the show end?

FERRIE. Tomorrow night.

COOPER. (*to* GLASON) Good news. You can still come and see it.

FERRIE. Discussions are ongoing.

COOPER. Miff here is my manager, Billy. Sorry. He didn't introduce himself properly did he? He's my manager. Mister fifteen per cent. It is still fifteen, isn't it Miff? Or has it gone up?

FERRIE. It has never gone up.

COOPER. And it's never come down. Has it?

FERRIE. Give me a drink.

(**GLASON** *pours* **FERRIE** *a drink.*)

COOPER. *(to GLASON)* Miff and I are locked into a sort of arranged marriage. On his terms. And he thinks there's no way I can get a divorce. Nice that he's out here with me though, isn't it? Nice that he's here to hold my hand when the show goes belly up. Isn't it, Billy? Really nice. Who do you think is paying? Who do you think is paying for Mr Miff Ferrie to come to Las Vegas USA and stay in a swanky hotel? Me. I'm paying. It's in the contract. That's right, isn't it Miff? The contract that you wrote specifies that you must be here with me and that I must pay.

FERRIE. I think we can get five thousand.

COOPER. Pounds?

FERRIE. Dollars. Payment due, plus compensation. And then on to New York. Nothing lost. I had a telegram today from Radio City and they are definitely interested – although the timings could get complicated.

COOPER. *(to GLASON)* Let me keep these two. And I'll see if I use any of the gags. You'll get paid as and when I do.

GLASON. How will I know?

COOPER. I'll tell you.

GLASON. Mr Cooper, I've been in this business more than thirty years.

COOPER. You don't trust me?

GLASON. I don't trust anyone.

COOPER. Good for you. My problem is I'm too trusting. Aren't I Miff?

(**FERRIE** *doesn't reply.*)

(To **GLASON***)* You know what Miff did before he started milking me? He was a singer.

FERRIE. You know what Tommy did before he met me? Nothing.

COOPER. 'Miff Ferrie and the Jackdauz' – J-a-c-k-d-a-u-z. Terrible isn't it? He can play the trombone as well. A man of many talents. *(To* **FERRIE***)* Billy sings too – you said that, didn't you? You should do a duet.

FERRIE. Where are you going?

*(***COOPER** *holds up the empty brandy bottle.)*

COOPER. Replenishments. You two have drunk all my liquor.

(Exit **COOPER***.)*

GLASON. He could call room service.

FERRIE. That would mean he'd have to tip the bellboy. Tommy doesn't like to tip.

Casino Floor – 1954

*(***GLASON** *walks towards the slot machine. He looks at it, jingles some change in his pocket and then walks away.)*

GLASON. I've met guys like Cooper before. He looks at me and sees the flip-side of the coin. Everything he's afraid of becoming.

Backstage Room – 1969

FERRIE. Tommy is a child. Like all performers. They need unconditional love, just like children. And even that is never enough. They need to punish you for loving them.

Onstage

(**COOPER** *in performance as before. Canned laughter at start, but it fades.*)

COOPER. *(laughs)* I'll never forget the war. I fought with the army. In the end I gave in and joined.

(Laughs. Paces about)

I got the military cross. Mind you, I got the navy a bit annoyed as well. *(Laughs)*

Like I said, I'm telling you a little bit more about myself this evening. I'd like to reveal my innermost being to you, ladies and gentlemen. *(Opens jacket)* Where's it gone? I had it here a moment a go.

Casino Floor – 1954

GLASON. I know how these things work. Believe me. I met a fella in a motel near Santa Fe one time who made the goddamn things.

Myth number one: that what has happened before affects what will happen next. Wrong! Each spin is independent.

Myth number two: if a machine pays out once it won't pay out again for a long time. Wrong! Like I say, each spin is independent.

Myth number three: the longer that a machine goes without paying out the jackpot the more likely it is to pay out with the next play. Wrong. Say it with me: each spin is independent.

Backstage Room – 1969

(**FERRIE** *dials the phone again.*)

FERRIE. – Gwen? You need to calm—

(*She rings off.*)

Casino Floor – 1954

GLASON. We all know that this is a game of odds. This whole ugly city is being built on games of odds that have only one winner. But we're only human. We can't help feeling that, you know… Only seventy per cent payout for two hours. No jackpot. And I feel… I just kinda feel that it's nearly time. Which I didn't feel when that lady was playing it just now. And I didn't feel when the guy was playing before her. But I do feel now. So… I don't know. What should I do?

The only golden rule – of course – is that you should never play these things when you actually need the money. That's the golden rule.

I had high hopes of Cooper. It felt like fate. To find him here. Knowing something about his act. Knowing that he needs gags by the yard.

I should have seen the show. Obviously. I'd talked the management into giving me a ticket. I'd done that. No sweat. But I, er, got caught up in a situation on the Black Jack table and, you know, there just wasn't a right time to leave. I couldn't find the moment. I was up at first, on a roll. It was beautiful. And after the way things had been going earlier – all goddamn day, actually, not just with cards but on the roulette wheel before that – well, I had to ride it. Didn't I? I had to. Until… The show was over. And my run was over. And I was, er, you know. My capabilities were much reduced. Cooper's tight. Like all these bigshots. They hate reaching for their wallets. He certainly won't pay three thousand. He probably won't even pay a grand.

Onstage

(By the end of this the canned laughter has dwindled to silence.)

COOPER. For my next trick I need a five pound note from the audience. *(Laughs)* Anyone got a five pound note? *(He asks the audience.)* Thank you very much. And I need a ten pound note from a member of the audience. Anyone got a ten pound note? Anyone? Thank you very much. And I need a twenty pound note from the audience. Anyone got a twenty pound note? Thank you very much indeed.

(He stuffs the notes into his pockets.) It's a disappearing trick – you'll never see them again. *(Laughs)*

(Paces about)

(To audience members) If you want it back after the show speak to my manager. Here's his card.

(Laughs) My manager's name is Mr Miff Ferrie. Quite a name. Quite a guy. He wasn't in the war. He was invalided out. They did a medical and found a great yellow streak down his back.

The Windermere Club – 1947

(As before. One week later.)

(COOPER is onstage.)

(FERRIE is watching attentively – although not laughing.)

(There is recorded laughter of about a dozen people – this is the band who have stayed to watch.)

(COOPER is mid-routine.)

COOPER. Now we have here four glass tumblers. *Un, deux,* three... And one plastic tray.

(Wobbles the tray) I don't know why I did that. *(Wobbles the tray again)* Good though, isn't it? *(Laughs)*

Now what I do, what I do… *(Laughs)* what I do is this. Are you watching? *(To offstage)* Is anyone watching? I can't see – the lights are in my eyes. *(Laughs)* What I do is I fill this one with water, and this one and that one – or should 'that' be 'this'? Never mind. I fill them all up and I put the plastic tray on like this.

(Wobbles the tray – but doesn't laugh) Wasn't funny that time. *(Laughs)*

Right. Are you still with me? I have six fresh eggs. These eggs are so fresh the hens haven't even missed them yet. Now I'd like someone here at random – you, with the curly trumpet. What's that, it's a called a sex – what? A saxophone! I see. Sorry. My hearing. *(Laughs)* Point at one of these eggs. Just one. This one? Are you sure? Really? You don't want to choose another? We'll use this one. *(Selects another)*

(Laughs)

Now what I'm going to do is this. I have four tubes. I put one tube there and another tube there like that and the other one there. So that's four tubes on four glasses – with a plastic tray in between them. *(Looks at his watch)* Haven't I finished yet?

(Laughs) Oh no, this is the good bit. Not this. The next bit. *(Laughs)* What I am going to do is go like this *(Mimes striking the tray)* or maybe like that… I haven't decided yet. And the tray will go over there – or over there. And the eggs will land in the water in the glasses.

(Paces, pulls a face)

(To offstage) Are you sure?

(To imagined audience) Move back a little please. I'm worried what will happens – when it goes wrong – I mean, if it goes wrong. *(Laughs)* You could catch them in your sex-thing. Saxophone.

Here we go now. The big trick. The climax of my act. One. Two. Two and a half.

(He hits the tray with the heel of his hand – the eggs land in the cups.)

*(*COOPER *accepts the applause and then looks back with mock-astonishment.)* They went into the…! The tray went over there and the eggs fell down… It worked! Just like that. It's never worked before! *(Laughs)*

(Bows)

(There is applause from the band.)

*(*FERRIE *stands.)*

FERRIE. *(to band)* Thanks boys. Thanks for staying on. Paul, make sure you practise that solo. And Nev, I want that cornet to be gleaming when you come back here tonight. See you all at seven.

(To COOPER*)* I thought you'd appreciate having an audience. If you can call ten musicians an audience.

COOPER. They seemed to like it.

FERRIE. Yes, well. It beats having to rehearse.

COOPER. Did you like it?

FERRIE. Mr Cooper—

COOPER. Call me Tommy.

FERRIE. Tommy, it's not so much a question of whether I liked it as whether the audience here at The Windermere Club would like it.

COOPER. And do you think they would?

FERRIE. Yes.

COOPER. Good.

FERRIE. They would certainly like it.

COOPER. Good.

FERRIE. The question is how much.

COOPER. How much would they like it?

FERRIE. Yes.

COOPER. Give me a chance and you'll find out. I mean, I appreciate you having me back for a second audition but what I really want is the chance to play here. Even just once. Let me show you what I can do.

FERRIE. The magic is definitely better than the impressions.

COOPER. Magic is what I love.

FERRIE. Well, I say magic…

    *(***COOPER** *laughs.)*

COOPER. I can do proper tricks.

FERRIE. I can see that.

COOPER. But I can also make people laugh.

FERRIE. I can see that, too. Tell me a little more about yourself Mr Cooper. Tommy.

COOPER. Well, Mr Ferrie, like a lot of people I'm not long out of the army. Were you in…?

    *(***FERRIE** *doesn't respond.* **COOPER** *continues.)*

So I've been working the circuit. Trying to make a name for myself.

FERRIE. Where have you played?

COOPER. The Manchester Hippodrome.

FERRIE. Really?

COOPER. And the Grand in Brighton. And the Playhouse, Weston-Super-Mare.

FERRIE. You've played those?

COOPER. Briefly. And I wasn't exactly top of the bill.

FERRIE. Or else why would you be here?

COOPER. And I had an audition for the BBC.

FERRIE. Radio?

    *(***COOPER** *laughs.)*

COOPER. Magic on the radio? *(***FERRIE** *doesn't respond)* No. Television. I think what I do could work very well on television.

FERRIE. How did it go? The audition.

COOPER. Er…

FERRIE. I don't recall seeing you.

COOPER. No.

FERRIE. Has the programme not gone out yet?

COOPER. No, they—

FERRIE. I have a set but I don't watch it very much, to be honest.

COOPER. They said I wasn't right for them at the moment.

FERRIE. *(sarcastic)* Oh?

COOPER. But I will be.

FERRIE. They said that?

COOPER. I know that.

FERRIE. I see. But you're prepared to bide your time here in the meantime?

COOPER. I'd love to play here.

FERRIE. Why the fez?

COOPER. Why not?

FERRIE. You've got good energy.

COOPER. Thank you.

FERRIE. And what I call 'attack'. I look for that in musicians and you've got that. You don't play trombone do you?

COOPER. No.

FERRIE. We're one trombone short.

COOPER. Ah.

FERRIE. What do you think of the floor show here?

COOPER. I...

FERRIE. How do you think your act would fit in?

COOPER. I haven't seen it.

FERRIE. You haven't seen the show?

COOPER. No.

FERRIE. Oh.

COOPER. Money's a bit tight, Mr Ferrie.

FERRIE. Is it.

COOPER. My wife and I don't get to go out particularly much.

FERRIE. I see.

COOPER. I'm sure it's very good.

FERRIE. You know who the main act is? The exotic Marqueez. You know her? You can probably guess the, er, drift of her act. Dance of the seven veils. Tasteful, if that's your taste. Would it trouble you to support that kind of act?

COOPER. No.

FERRIE. Would it worry your wife?

COOPER. No.

FERRIE. Do you have a manager?

COOPER. No.

FERRIE. You'll need one.

COOPER. Will I?

FERRIE. When you get on television.

COOPER. Are you going to give me a chance, Mr Ferrie?

FERRIE. I'll give you a week.

COOPER. Okay.

FERRIE. That suits you?

COOPER. Yes.

FERRIE. Come by tomorrow and we'll sort out the details.

COOPER. Thank you.

FERRIE. Two things.

COOPER. What?

FERRIE. In the war – you asked me what I did in the war.

COOPER. Did I?

FERRIE. I was musical advisor to the USO. I wasn't lucky enough to be able to fight.

COOPER. Right.

FERRIE. Or fit enough.

COOPER. And the other thing?

FERRIE. I'm not sure about the fez.

Onstage

(**COOPER** *in performance as before, now with a pack of cards.*)

COOPER. Would you think of any card in the pack, sir, at random. Don't say it, just think it. Don't say it! Can you do that? This is mind over matter. If you don't mind, I don't matter.

(He has a dipping duck prop.)

I put the cards in there... Now this duck will take your chosen card from that pack. Now you may have seen a duck do that before. But be fair...blindfolded?! *(He ties a scarf around the duck's face.)* What was your card, sir?

(Reply from the audience. Cooper looks at the card the duck has chosen.)

Correct. *(He throws the card away without showing anyone.)*

Now, I don't like to talk about myself, really. Some people do, don't they? But I'm not one of those people. And I don't like being interviewed. Hang on a minute, I've forgotten something. Oh yes. I'm supposed to be telling jokes.

(Laughs) I went to the doctor this morning. I said, doctor, I can't say my 'F's or my 'T's. He said, 'Well you can't say fairer than that.'

(Laughs) I've got a confession to make. Ready? *(To offstage)* Do you think they're ready?

(Paces) Actually I've got two confessions.

First confession...

(Stops – counts on fingers) Actually I've got three confessions. Are you ready? I'm not. *(Laughs)*

First confession: I sometimes hit the wife. Shall I do a magic trick?

(He takes a bottle of whiskey, a glass and two metal cylinders – pours himself a large drink and downs it.)

Cheers!

(He pours another and downs it.)

Double cheers!

Right.

Now then.

Bottle – glass. Glass – bottle. *(Laughs)* Yes, I have on more than one occasion hit my wife. *(To offstage)* Maybe this is why I don't like to talk about myself! *(Laughs)* It's not her fault. How could it be? I love her. But I lose my temper. What's that – is there a punchline? No sir. There isn't. Or was that your idea of a joke?

Glass – bottle. Bottle – glass.

Second confession. *(Laughs)* I warned you. *(Laughs)* I drink too much.

(Pours himself another drink and downs it.)

Those two confessions may well be related. And my third confession – almost done now, madam, don't worry – my third confession is that there is another lady in my life. Yes, sir – in 'that' way. And I love her very much, too. Do I hit her…?

(To offstage) I told you this wouldn't work. Didn't I? I told them, ladies and gentlemen. I told them you wouldn't find this funny. But they said I was always funny. They said they laugh whatever you say.

(Laughs)

Bottle – glass.

(Harrumphs)

Sorry. I hope you don't mind, ladies and gentlemen. I hope you don't mind. This is me. Here I am. Love me or loathe me. Take me or leave me. Laugh or bleedin' cry. Who's crying?

(Wipes a tear from his eye)

Who's crying?!

(Takes out a hankie and sobs)

(Stands)

(Laughs)

Bottle – glass. Glass – bottle.

ACT TWO

(The stage set as before.)

Casino Floor – 1954

*(**GLASON** is pacing up and down.)*

GLASON. If I can get a thousand bucks from Cooper, I'll be OK. That will sort me out and set me up. Trouble is, it's getting harder. You know? I've pretty much sold as many copies as I can over here. And if Cooper ties up the UK market then I… I'll need to find a new income stream.

(He looks back at the slot machine.)

Maybe I should get back on stage. Christ, if I don't manage to make a sale to Cooper, I might have to. Just to earn a few bucks. Just to get home. Why not? Why shouldn't I?

This, er, Irish guy goes into a bar. He's from Boston, like me. Any Bostonians in the audience tonight? OK. Never mind. So this Irish fella goes into a bar and he's got a stetson on. He's wearing a stetson! A ten gallon hat. And he goes into the bar. Which is in Texas. Sorry. I should have mentioned that. This Irish Bostonian guy in a hat goes into a bar in Texas. Dallas or Houston. Wherever. And he says— shit. No. He's a Texan. That's why he's wearing the hat. And the bar is in Boston… I think.

A Train Carriage – 1969

*(**MARY** has a bow tie that has been cut in three pieces –
she is sewing velcro to put it back together.)*

MARY. There's nowhere quite like a train on a Sunday
evening. Is there?

*(She takes a deep breath, composing herself. Trying not
to cry.)*

I like to get a carriage to myself. If I can. So that
there's space for the cases and also no need to chit
chat. A woman travelling alone can seem an inviting
proposition for a certain type of man. Or, actually, for
just about any man in my experience.

Of course, when Tommy is travelling with me he likes
the privacy of a carriage. He needs it. Can't be spending
three hours to Crewe signing autographs and saying
'Just like that' to everyone and their mother. 'Keep
them away, Mary' he says to me. 'Just keep them away.'

It also gives me space to work on whatever I need to
work on. Sewing hidden pockets into trousers. A tie
that's twenty feet long and just keeps unravelling. This.
(Holds up bow-tie).

No one realises how much time Tommy puts into
preparation. All magicians have to. Everything has to
be just right, so that it can go wrong just as he wants
it to. He looks chaotic, shambolic but it's all planned.
Everything is planned. Even the improvisation,

God, this train is slow. We're crawling away from
London. I'd like to feel speed. Isn't it supposed to
be the age of technology? Everything goes fast now
doesn't it? Why do trains still have to be so slow?

And the buffet car is closed. And I haven't had a cup
of tea since this morning and what I could actually do
with is a drink. A proper drink. I would really like a
drink.

Casino Floor – 1954

(**GLASON** *walks up to the slot machine.*)

GLASON. At least the machine is fair. It doesn't judge you. It doesn't cheat you. It doesn't favour the guy in the smart suit or the girl with the tight-fitting sweater. It doesn't care if you're a Jew or an Italian or even if you're, I don't know, French. The machine doesn't care. It will still pay out. It will still obey the odds. Although, from your point of view, odds don't feel like something mathematical, they don't feel like probability, they feel like luck. Which is much more personal. Much more loaded. It's about getting what you deserve. Or not getting it. So putting a dollar in the slot becomes a conversation with fate. With a very pure, scientific judgement of whether, that particular moment you are lucky or not. Do I feel lucky?

Restaurant – 1969

(*Enter* **MIFF FERRIE**. *He sits at the table with* **COOPER**.)

COOPER. You're looking well.

FERRIE. Thank you.

COOPER. Seriously.

FERRIE. Okay.

COOPER. What do you fancy?

FERRIE. What's good?

COOPER. Everything's good, Miff. I wouldn't take you out anywhere sub-standard, would I?

FERRIE. Of course not.

COOPER. Have whatever you like.

(**FERRIE** *looks at the menu.*)

(**COOPER** *keeps on looking at* **FERRIE**.)

(**FERRIE** *puts the menu down.*)

FERRIE. Is this about Gwen?

COOPER. What? Gwen?

FERRIE. I thought perhaps that you wanted to speak to me about…

COOPER. She sends her regards, by the way. Gwen does. She wanted to be here but we couldn't get a babysitter.

FERRIE. I'm not going to pretend, Tommy.

COOPER. Pretend what?

FERRIE. That I don't know…certain things.

COOPER. What things, Miff?

*(***FERRIE*** doesn't reply.)*

COOPER. This is about us, Miff. This meal. Me taking you out for dinner. It's about us.

FERRIE. Sorting things out?

COOPER. If you want to put it like that.

FERRIE. How would you put it?

COOPER. I had the sense that you weren't happy.

FERRIE. Did you?

COOPER. You've been very uptight, Miff. Even more than usual.

FERRIE. Right.

COOPER. You're on my case about everything.

FERRIE. That's not true.

COOPER. Wanting to know my every move.

FERRIE. I just want bookings and remittances to go through me. That's all. Anyone else in my position would want the same.

COOPER. It's getting to me, Miff.

FERRIE. So follow the rules.

COOPER. Follow the rules?

FERRIE. Yes.

COOPER. You think I've got it pretty easy, don't you?

FERRIE. No.

COOPER. You do. Everyone does. They think I'm the luckiest sod alive.

(He finishes his drink and looks around for a waiter.)

COOPER. Waiter!

FERRIE. I don't think that.

COOPER. What did Gwen tell you?

FERRIE. She called me.

COOPER. I know.

FERRIE. A couple of weeks ago.

COOPER. I know.

(A silence.)

COOPER. What did she tell you?

FERRIE. I think you know what she told me.

COOPER. Do I?

FERRIE. Yes.

COOPER. She feels the pressure, too, Miff. Course she does. Two kids to bring up. Me away a lot. She soaks it up like a fucking sponge but it gets to her from time to time.

FERRIE. Tommy, you can't do what you—

COOPER. *(interrupting)* She hates you.

FERRIE. Tommy…

COOPER. Thinks you're ripping me off. I have to defend you to her. Can you believe that? I defend you! *(Laughs)* *(Looking around)* Waiter! What do you have to do to get a fucking drink round here?

What did she say to you Miff? What did she say?

FERRIE. She said that you had… She said that you had hit her.

COOPER. Did she?

FERRIE. In front of the children.

COOPER. She said that?

FERRIE. Yes.

COOPER. Was she drunk?

FERRIE. No.

COOPER. Are you sure?

FERRIE. Tommy, I know Gwen and I—

COOPER. *(interrupting)* How did she sound? How did she come across?

FERRIE. She was…

COOPER. Hysterical.

FERRIE. She was very upset.

COOPER. And she said that? She said that I'd—

FERRIE. Yes.

COOPER. So what did you say? Had she called the police? Or did you? Did you call the police, Miff? Christ, I've been so busy I've hardly known what day of the week it is but I don't remember the police coming round.

FERRIE. I didn't call the police.

COOPER. Maybe they're still looking for me. *(Hides behind menu)*

FERRIE. I tried to calm her down.

COOPER. Tough job. Been there. Done that. Got the scars.

FERRIE. It's not acceptable, Tommy.

COOPER. Do you think she's seeing someone else?

FERRIE. What?

COOPER. Maybe she's trying to throw me off the scent. Create a diversion. *(Laughs)* Only kidding.

FERRIE. Does she know about…you?

COOPER. What do you mean?

FERRIE. *(pause)* You and Mary.

COOPER. Which Mary?

FERRIE. You know which Mary.

(**COOPER** *slams his glass down on the table.*)

COOPER. I'm dying of thirst here!

FERRIE. I don't want to get involved in your personal life, Tommy.

COOPER. Er…!

FERRIE. I didn't ask Gwen to phone me.

COOPER. You really should have called the police.

FERRIE. But I can't ignore what she said.

COOPER. If you think what she said is true.

FERRIE. And I can't ignore what I can see with my own eyes.

COOPER. Or are you going to do a citizens' arrest?

FERRIE. You need to get a grip.

COOPER. *(holding out his hands as if cuffed)* Take me, I won't put up a struggle.

FERRIE. It's bad for business.

(A silence. And then COOPER *laughs.)*

COOPER. Bad for business?

FERRIE. You need to protect your reputation.

COOPER. Poor old Gwen, phones you up thinking she'll get some sympathy for whatever afflictions she's dreamt up for herself and all you're thinking is that it might be bad for business.

FERRIE. You know what I meant.

COOPER. That it might cost you money!

*(*FERRIE *stands.)*

FERRIE. One day you will appreciate what I've done for you.

COOPER. Sit down.

FERRIE. You can buy yourself out of our arrangement any time you like.

COOPER. Sit down.

FERRIE. You can.

COOPER. Look, here comes a fucking waiter.

FERRIE. But you don't.

COOPER. Finally.

FERRIE. So you must think I'm worth something.

*(*COOPER *holds a hand up to the waiter.)*

COOPER. You're a treasure, Miff. And a cunt. And I love you like a brother. Now, what are you having?

Train Carriage – 1969

(**MARY**, *as before*)

MARY. Sometimes it doesn't seem real. Even on a day like this, after what has happened, after what he has been like, I still have to pinch myself. Travelling the country. Preparing his props. Making sure everything is set up properly. That he's got everything. I sort things out with the band too.

The people I have met! You wouldn't believe it. Benny Hill. Eric Sykes. Jimmy Edwards. It's become normal for me. And it's different from before, when I was one of the crew in the studio. Now I'm his right-hand gal.

Sometimes I wish I could go on stage with him. As an assistant maybe. A glamorous assistant in a sparkly leotard, fishnet stockings and high heeled patent leather boots. If Tommy were a magician, if he just did magic, then I could. But he doesn't need anyone else. Not up there. He doesn't need a straight man or a stooge. I wouldn't mind being his stooge. *(Laughs)* Maybe that's exactly what I am.

I've met Frankie Howerd. Bruce Forsyth. Anyone you can think of. Not at a run of the mill gig like this one will be, but at the big shows – the Royal Variety and for TV.

I did ask him once if I could sing. Before his act. Or after the interval. I can sing.

(Sings, softly)

"NOW IS THE HOUR
WHEN WE MUST SAY GOODBYE.
SOON YOU'LL BE SAILING
FAR ACROSS THE SEA."

They all love Tommy. All the big stars. They know how good he is. And he loves me. He really, really loves me. And I love him. Even when I shouldn't. Even when it hurts.

(Sings)

"WHILE YOU'RE AWAY
OH, THEN, REMEMBER ME.
WHEN YOU RETURN
YOU'LL FIND ME WAITING HERE."

Onstage

(**COOPER** *onstage in performance as before, with the bottles and glass.*)

COOPER. It makes sense for a man to have two wives. Wait – I know what you're thinking sir. Two?! Hear me out. I am not a lunatic. Two wives?! *(Laughs)* All I'm saying is that a man is different at home and at work. And has different needs. So we need a different woman. One to look after the family and the home and to hassle us about all the things we haven't done and all the love we haven't shown them. And one to have sex with. *(Laughs)* I'm joking. *(To offstage)* I have to tell them when I'm joking, now.

This lady down here is giving me the evil eye. *(Laughs)* What was that? How many times did it happen? How many times did what happen? Oh. The lady with the sour face wants to know how many times, er…the thing with my wife, the lovely Gwen, "Dove", to me… None of your business. Is it? Is it? She's gone all silent. You don't know anything about me. You don't know anything about my wife. So, er… Ha! She's walking out, ladies and gentlemen. Yes, go on sir, you go with her. And give her a belt round the chops from me! *(Laughs)* Did I just say that?

Hotel Room – 1954

(March 1954. The Las Vegas hotel room as before. Moments later.)

GLASON. So he hates to tip. And he hates paying writers. And he hates paying you.

FERRIE. You're not seeing him at his best.

GLASON. I've seen worse.

FERRIE. After a show. Having had a drink.

GLASON. Or two.

FERRIE. And asking him for money.

GLASON. I wasn't asking him for money. I was offering goods for sale.

FERRIE. You know what he does when get gets a cab?

GLASON. No.

FERRIE. Instead of a tip, you know what he does?

GLASON. No.

FERRIE. He puts a teabag in their top pocket. I've seen him do it. *(Impersonating* **COOPER***)* 'Have a drink on me.'

GLASON. Nice.

FERRIE. *(still impersonating* **COOPER** *– laughs)* 'Have a drink on me.' You think he needs new material?

GLASON. Everyone needs new material.

FERRIE. But you think Tommy does?

GLASON. Well…

FERRIE. The show's not closing because of him.

GLASON. No, but…

FERRIE. What?

GLASON. Have they asked him to stay on alone?

FERRIE. He's part of the show.

GLASON. But they could have given him a spot somewhere else. Couldn't they?

FERRIE. We're going to New York.

GLASON. Have they invited him back?

FERRIE. For what?

GLASON. A solo show.

FERRIE. They might do.

GLASON. Have they said that?

FERRIE. What are you getting at?

GLASON. Nothing.

FERRIE. What did you think of the show?

GLASON. Which show?

FERRIE. Our show.

GLASON. Your show?

FERRIE. Tommy.

(**GLASON** *hesitates.*)

FERRIE. You did see the show didn't you?

GLASON. *(pause)* Er…yes.

FERRIE. So what did you think of it?

GLASON. I thought it wasn't a show that would run and run.

FERRIE. Why?

GLASON. Well, Vera Lynn, obviously.

FERRIE. She was a mistake.

GLASON. She means nothing to folks over here.

FERRIE. So I'm told.

GLASON. And she moves kind of, you know, heavily.

FERRIE. What about the other acts?

GLASON. Which ones?

FERRIE. Any of them.

GLASON. *(pause)* They didn't make much impression.

FERRIE. And Tommy?

GLASON. Brilliant.

FERRIE. Be honest.

GLASON. Very smooth prestidigitations.

FERRIE. OK.

GLASON. And very funny.

FERRIE. He got a lot of laughs.

GLASON. The audience loved him. I loved him. But…there was something missing.

FERRIE. Like what?

GLASON. He needed more material.

FERRIE. More jokes?

GLASON. Absolutely. More jokes. He felt like he just didn't have enough ammunition. And the crowds over here demand it.

FERRIE. Do you think there was too much magic?

GLASON. Yes.

FERRIE. Tommy loves magic.

GLASON. We all love magic.

FERRIE. He can't get enough of it.

GLASON. Everyone loves magic!

FERRIE. But comedy-magic?

GLASON. That all depends.

FERRIE. On what?

GLASON. The comedy.

FERRIE. You don't think he's funny enough?

GLASON. He's incredibly funny.

FERRIE. I don't want him to be seen as some kind of novelty act.

GLASON. But you can always be funnier.

FERRIE. How well do you know Las Vegas?

GLASON. Pretty well.

FERRIE. You think it's got a future?

GLASON. Have you seen how many hotels they're building?

FERRIE. Casinos, you mean.

GLASON. The two go together.

FERRIE. Perhaps. But do they need entertainment?

GLASON. Of course. No one can gamble all day every day. Well, there's enough people who can't.

FERRIE. I'm not sure. It's such a long way from anywhere.

GLASON. That's the beauty of it. The escapism. Big hotels, high stakes gambling, big stars on stage. It's a winning combination. Once they get the construction work finished it's going to be a new vaudeville, right here in the desert. And you're looking at someone who played on the old vaudeville so I know of what I speak.

FERRIE. And you think Tommy needs to be funnier?

GLASON. I never said that.

FERRIE. You think he should buy your books.

GLASON. I know what I'm doing, Mr Ferrie. I work with the top guys.

FERRIE. Who else is doing comedy magic?

GLASON. No one that I work with.

FERRIE. Generally.

GLASON. Carl Ballantine.

FERRIE. Anyone else?

GLASON. Robert Orben.

FERRIE. I know the names.

GLASON. Those are the two biggest.

FERRIE. And how similar are they to Tommy?

GLASON. Hard to say. They probably both have a little more material. Ballantine was on Ed Sullivan's show last year. You know Ed? He uses my stuff. I could introduce you. Now that's where you want to be. On TV.

FERRIE. We've done a bit.

GLASON. There's an explosion. Ed Sullivan. Milt Berle's show. You ever seen that?

(**FERRIE** *shakes his head.*)

GLASON. It's been a whole new lease of life for these guys. And the acts they put on. I could speak to Milt, too. You're going to New York, you say?

FERRIE. Nothing's finalised.

GLASON. Any shows lined up?

FERRIE. No.

GLASON. You get Mr Cooper on stage in New York, I'll get people in to see him. Guaranteed. TV people. That's the way things are going, Mr Ferrie. Television. I don't know about England but over here it's blowing everything else out of the water.

FERRIE. I thought you said the future was here in Las Vegas.

GLASON. Las Vegas for a vacation, at home on the couch watching TV for the other fifty-one weeks of the year. But of course it consumes material. Chews it up. Can't just use the same gags time after time like you could in my day. You need new stuff. And on TV you've got to be quick. You've got to have gags flying like that. I am willing to negotiate, by the way.

FERRIE. About what?

GLASON. The books. And it would be tax deductible.

FERRIE. I've got your card?

GLASON. I'd love to help you both. Any way that I can. Tell you what. For a cash downpayment right now, I'll let you keep these two. And then I'll send the others on to New York or London or wherever.

FERRIE. How much?

GLASON. Five hundred dollars.

(**TOMMY COOPER** *returns with a bottle of brandy.*)

FERRIE. You'll have to speak to Tommy.

Onstage

(**COOPER** *performing, as before. He is now drunk.*)

(*He is still doing the bottle-glass routine.*)

COOPER. You know, I'm on a whisky diet. I've lost three days already. (*Laughs, darkly*)

I went to the doctor the other day and he said "You've got hypochondria." I said "Not that as well"

Bottle-glass. Glass-bottle. *(Lifts the metal containers)* Here's the bottle and here's the glass. The bottle will now change places with the glass.

(To offstage) They're not laughing.

Bottle-glass. Glass-bottle.

(Shouting offstage) They're not fucking laughing!

Don't you know who I am? Don't you know how funny I am? Eh? I only have to stand here and people will laugh.

(He stands)

Why aren't you laughing? Why aren't you laughing?!

(Switches the two canisters. Peers under them)

(Paces, laughs)

Do you know how hard this is? Being up here? Do you have any idea? You just want me to be funny. That's all. Nothing else. Do you think I'm a fucking machine?

(To offstage) They're still not laughing

The bottle has now changed places with the glass. The difficult part is to make them go back again.

(Lifts the canisters again, and the bottle and glass have changed places.)

Just like that.

Restaurant – 1969

*(**COOPER** is still at the table, eating dessert. And still drinking. **MARY** arrives. He ignores her.)*

MARY. Hello.

COOPER. He left early. Miff the muff. *(Laughs)*

MARY. Right.

COOPER. Said he doesn't like rich food in the middle of the day. "It disagrees with me."

MARY. It's time to go.

COOPER. How did you know I would be here?

MARY. I called Miff. After you left me standing in the street.

COOPER. Nice dress.

MARY. Thank you.

COOPER. Where did you get it?

MARY. You bought it for me.

COOPER. Did I?

MARY. In York.

COOPER. Really?

MARY. Yes. It was in a sale.

COOPER. It's, er, figure-hugging.

MARY. That's the fashion.

COOPER. Not sure I like you wearing it out and about, though.

MARY. Tommy…

COOPER. Don't want everyone seeing your—

MARY. Tommy! We need to get to the station.

(A beat)

COOPER. I missed you today.

MARY. I saw you this morning.

COOPER. I missed you.

MARY. We need to go.

COOPER. Come here.

*(**MARY** goes to him and he hugs her.)*

COOPER. Where are we going?

MARY. Preston.

COOPER. Fuck.

MARY. Come on.

COOPER. I wish I could take the week off.

MARY. To do what?

COOPER. I can think of a few things.

MARY. Tommy, people will see us.

COOPER. I wish I didn't have to go to Preston.

Train Carriage – 1969

(**MARY**, *as before.*)

MARY. They warned me he was difficult. Before I even met him. The TV people warned me. I was working there, on the production team, and they warned me he was even more difficult than the rest. Which he was. Arrived late, his chauffeur walking ahead of him with his bags. But everyone could see the talent, the focus.

We, er, 'did it' in his dressing room. The first time. And then other times. And that was how it started. I felt like the luckiest girl in London.

I became his personal assistant. Very personal. When he's not rehearsing or recording a TV show we're usually on the road. And I look after things. Him. And the show. Food is the biggest challenge. He's difficult with food. So I've got a camping stove and I'll cook up one of his favourites – lamb chops or a steak – right there in our dressing room. If I didn't, I swear, he wouldn't eat half the time. He'd forget.

I don't get paid. Not a salary. But, you know, he looks after me. And I've been married already. Had kids. I don't need to do that again. I prefer this. This is an adventure. If it's Monday, it must be Preston. Or it will be.

Hotel Room – 1954

(*The Las Vegas hotel room as before. Moments later.*)

COOPER. You still here?

GLASON. I was just leaving.

COOPER. Not you, him. (*indicating* **FERRIE**)

(**COOPER** *pours himself a large drink.*)

COOPER. What is it that you need to ask me?

(**GLASON** *hesitates.*)

COOPER. What have you two been talking about?

FERRIE. Nothing.

COOPER. What have you been cooking up?

FERRIE. Nothing.

COOPER. You're like a couple of naughty schoolboys.

GLASON. We were talking about comedy. Television. The opportunities.

COOPER. Opportunities?

GLASON. I was saying to Mr Ferrie that it would be good if you could maybe do a show in New York.

COOPER. We're going back to England.

FERRIE. Via New York.

GLASON. It would be good for people to see you. Even if it was just one night. You could do a special show. Make sure all the right people were there. It wouldn't be too difficult to arrange.

COOPER. Hang on a moment.

GLASON. What?

COOPER. Are you trying to be my bloody agent now?

GLASON. No!

COOPER. Are you hearing this, Miff? Are you listening to what he's saying? *(To* **GLASON***)* So you want to take over from Miff?

GLASON. Of course not.

COOPER. I don't mind.

GLASON. I'm not an agent. Or a manager. Or anything like that.

COOPER. Neither was Miff before he met me. Were you, Miff? All you've got to do is get your claws into some talent and away you go. Isn't that right, Miff? And the truth is, the time could be right for me to make a change. You know? Miff and I have this sort of hate–hate relationship so quite frankly I'm open to offers.

FERRIE. Tommy…

COOPER. Let's hear what the man has to say, Miff. Let's hear him out. Go on, Billy. What's your proposal?

GLASON. I don't have a proposal. I was just suggesting that there are some people in New York who might like to see your show.

COOPER. What people?

GLASON. TV people.

COOPER. TV people. He knows TV people, Miff. Carry on. I'm all ears. *(Laughs)* What percentage would you want?

GLASON. I don't want any percentage.

COOPER. Where do I sign?

GLASON. For God's sake.

FERRIE. Tommy you're behaving like an ass.

COOPER. He says he doesn't want to take a percentage. What do you think about that?

FERRIE. You're drunk.

COOPER. You're bleeding me dry.

FERRIE. You haven't paid me a penny for two months.

COOPER. Who's paying for you to be here?

FERRIE. That's different.

COOPER. Is it?

FERRIE. I don't want to talk about this now.

COOPER. Neither do I. You can talk to my lawyer.

GLASON. I'm done.

COOPER. G'night.

GLASON. *(to* **FERRIE***)* Goodnight.

> **(GLASON** *goes to pick up the books but* **COOPER** *lifts them away.)*

COOPER. You can pick them up in the morning.

GLASON. No way.

COOPER. I need time to take a proper look.

GLASON. No.

COOPER. You're asking for an awful lot of money.

GLASON. Pay a deposit.

COOPER. Tomorrow.

GLASON. Now.

> (**COOPER** *turns away, looking at the books.* **GLASON** *looks to* **FERRIE**, *who shrugs.*)

GLASON. How do I know that you won't steal the best material?

COOPER. Steal your stolen gags? (*Laughs*)

> (*A silence. And then* **GLASON** *shakes* **FERRIE**'s *hand.*)

GLASON. Nice meeting you.

> (*Exit* **GLASON**.)

FERRIE. He was trying to help us.

COOPER. He was trying to sell his encyclopedias.

> (**COOPER** *sits down on the bed, pours himself another drink and starts to study the books properly.*)

> (**FERRIE** *finishes his own drink.*)

FERRIE. This doesn't have to be bad for us.

COOPER. The show closing? No, it's a triumph.

FERRIE. We've got forty weeks a year guaranteed back home.

COOPER. Whoopee.

FERRIE. But we need to work together. Amicably. If we're going to get to where we want to be. I'm not asking you to like me.

COOPER. Good.

FERRIE. But I do need you to appreciate what I've done and what I'm doing.

COOPER. You need to be loved.

FERRIE. No.

COOPER. Just leave me alone.

FERRIE. Tommy…

COOPER. Please.

> (*A silence*)

FERRIE. Are you okay?

COOPER. I will be the moment you get out of my room. I'm tired, Miff.

FERRIE. Then go to bed.

(**FERRIE** *takes the books from him and puts them on the bedside cabinet.*)

COOPER. You're not my mother.

(**FERRIE** *takes the glass and the bottle and puts them in the bedside cabinet.*)

FERRIE. Everything's going to be fine.

COOPER. I won't miss the audiences here.

FERRIE. No.

COOPER. Half-dead, mostly.

FERRIE. And smarting from having lost their savings playing blackjack.

COOPER. I've had to work bloody hard.

FERRIE. And you've done a great job.

COOPER. There's not the same connection I'm used to.

FERRIE. You've been marvellous.

COOPER. They don't know me.

FERRIE. You've had to start from scratch out here.

COOPER. They seemed to like me, though.

FERRIE. They loved you. You should have heard what people were saying at the interval tonight.

COOPER. What were they saying?

FERRIE. How great you were and how they hoped you were coming back in the second half.

COOPER. They were all right in the end.

FERRIE. You won them over.

COOPER. So we're going to New York?

FERRIE. Don't worry about that now.

COOPER. I should send Gwen a telegram.

FERRIE. Tomorrow.

COOPER. Let her know when we're likely to be home.

FERRIE. I'll do it.

COOPER. Would you?

FERRIE. Of course.

(COOPER *yawns.*)

COOPER. I'm knackered.

FERRIE. Go to bed.

(COOPER *lies down on the bed.*)

FERRIE. I'll see you in the morning.

(*Exit* FERRIE.)

(*After a moment* COOPER *sits up.*)

(*He gets the drink and his glass out of the cabinet, and then gets the books.*)

COOPER. (*reading*) 'He wasn't bald. His head just grew up through his hair.' He wasn't bald. (*Laughs*) His head just grew up through his hair.

(*He downs his first drink and then picks up the phone.*)

(*On the phone*) – Hello, yes. I'd like to send a telegram. My wife.

How much will it cost?

For the whole thing?

Per letter?! (*American accent*) Forget about it.

(*Puts the phone down*)

Casino Floor – 1954

(GLASON *reaches into his pockets and pulls out a handful of dollars.*)

(*He walks straight over to the slot machine and puts them in.*)

(*Soon he has nothing left.*)

GLASON. You see, the thing you've got to remember about a slot machine is that each spin is independent from the one before and the one after. So you can watch a machine for hours or for minutes or not at all and it doesn't make the blindest bit of difference.

And the other thing you've got to remember is that it's not about you. The machine doesn't care about you. So don't take it personally.

(He kicks the machine and curses.)

(A beat)

Can you lend me five bucks? You know, just to… This thing is aching to pay out. It's bulging at the goddamn seams! Or just a dollar. I'll split the winnings with you fifty-fifty. Just a dollar? My luck's about to change.

You know what my problem is? Nothing to do with luck. Nothing to do with talent, neither. I'm just too nice. Too damn nice to get on in this world.

Restaurant – 1969

(MARY and COOPER in the restaurant as before.)

COOPER. I've had a bloody awful day.

MARY. Come on.

COOPER. Horrible.

MARY. You can forget all about it.

COOPER. You've no idea.

MARY. Have you got a coat?

COOPER. I said you've no idea.

MARY. And have you paid?

(COOPER grabs her wrists. MARY looks around to check if anyone is watching)

COOPER. You not listening to me.

MARY. I am now.

COOPER. I've had a bad day.

MARY. I know.

COOPER. You don't know! Bloody hell! What is it with women?

MARY. Tell me…

COOPER. Why do they think they've heard it all before?

MARY. But we need to catch our train.

COOPER. That's all you care about, isn't it? Trains. Hotels. Theatres. Clubs.

MARY. Tommy.

COOPER. You know how I like to spend my Sundays don't you?

MARY. Yes.

COOPER. Tell me. If you know, tell me.

MARY. At home.

COOPER. With who?

(**MARY** *doesn't reply.*)

COOPER. With who? Can't you bear to say her name?

MARY. With Gwen. And your children.

COOPER. That's right. Every Sunday, that's what I like to do. Every Sunday. No matter where I have to travel to, no matter where I am travelling to the next day – whether it's Liverpool or Blackpool or sodding Preston I like to go home for a Sunday roast cooked by Dove, for me. That's what I like to do.

MARY. Why didn't you do that today?

COOPER. Good question.

(*A beat.* **MARY** *tries to pull her hands away but* **COOPER** *won't let her.*)

COOPER. You look like a tart in that dress. You look like a bloody tart.

(*He lets go of her wrists.*)

I need to get away from Miff. He's been very aggressive with Dove. Very threatening. I think he thinks that he can put pressure on me through her. Not nice. Not nice at all.

MARY. Why don't you leave them both?

COOPER. What?

MARY. You're always talking about it. Why don't you just do it?

COOPER. I never talk about leaving my wife.

MARY. But you say you want to be with me. You say you can't stand being apart from me.

COOPER. Keep your voice down.

MARY. Leave them both. Do it.

COOPER. We're in a public place.

MARY. Or are you scared?

(**COOPER** *laughs.*)

MARY. Are you actually scared, Thomas?

COOPER. Of what?

MARY. I don't know.

COOPER. Of Miff?

MARY. Maybe.

COOPER. Or of my wife? You think I'm scared of my wife?

(**MARY** *shrugs.*)

COOPER. Or do you think I'm scared of you?

(*He laughs and makes another grab for her wrist but she pulls away.*)

MARY. I think you're scared of yourself.

COOPER. Myself?

MARY. Yes. Perhaps. I don't know.

COOPER. If I could leave Miff, I would. My lawyer is working on it.

MARY. Right.

COOPER. It's complicated.

MARY. Yes.

COOPER. But I'll never leave Dove.

MARY. No.

COOPER. I never will.

MARY. What if you had to choose?

COOPER. Choose what?

MARY. But I don't even mean that.

COOPER. Don't mean what?

MARY. I don't want you to leave your wife.

COOPER. I never will.

MARY. Or your agent.

COOPER. Little Scottish…

MARY. I just want… I love you so much, Thomas.

COOPER. I know.

MARY. But I feel like we're in hiding.

COOPER. That's the choice you made. I've always been clear about—

MARY. Not us, really. Although we are. The ridiculous charade of me being your assistant. Who books a double room with his assistant?! But it's not that.

COOPER. Mary, you don't know—

MARY. It feels like you're in hiding from the whole world.

COOPER. Fuck the train…

MARY. You're never honest.

COOPER. Fuck Preston…

MARY. You're never yourself.

COOPER. …I'm going home.

MARY. Back to Dove.

COOPER. Yes.

MARY. Maybe she'll be able to heat up some roast beef and Yorkshire pudding for you.

COOPER. I'll see you tomorrow.

MARY. It's the real you on stage. In a way. Even though it's an act. That's the funny thing. You're most yourself when you're most hidden away.

COOPER. Be careful with the bags on the train.

MARY. I do love you though.

COOPER. Don't lose anything.

MARY. I'll never stop loving you.

(**MARY** *goes over to kiss him. He half lets her.*)

COOPER. And I don't want to see you in that dress again.

Backstage Room – 1969

(**MIFF FERRIE** *is on the phone.*)

FERRIE. – Yes, dear.

No, dear.

(**FERRIE** *covers the phone.*)

(*To the audience, stage whisper*) My wife.

Any moment now, dear.

Because I'm on the phone to you, dear.

I will.

I won't.

I might…

(*Swiftly*) Okay, no, I won't.

Indeed.

Love you too, dear.

(*He puts the phone down.*)

Sometimes… You know, late at night. Sometimes I wonder how things might have turned out if I'd carried on performing. We were good. We were big – quite big. We could have been big. If we'd had the right breaks. Ah well.

(*He picks up his coat and briefcase and turns off the light.*)

Hotel Room – 1954

(**COOPER** *in the hotel room as before, moments later.*)

(*He picks the phone up again.*)

It's me again. About the telegram. I want to send one.
Cooper. Tommy Cooper.

My wife's contact details are in your files.

Ready?

'Show over – STOP – Coming home'

Yes, that's all.

Wait. 'Show over – STOP – Coming home – STOP –
Love you'

How much is that?

I'll send down the shirt of my back as well.

(*He puts the phone down. Pours himself another drink*)

COOPER. *(pacing)* He wasn't bald…

(*Laughs*)

I met this man once – he wasn't bald… He wasn't!
His head just grew up through his hair. And I said to
him, I did, I said I missed my catnap today. I slept right
through it. *(Pause)* You know, it's not my day. I backed
a horse at twenty to one and it came in at twenty past
four. So I bought a greyhound. A friend of mine said
what are you gonna do with it? I said, race it. He said,
by the look of that dog I think you'll beat it *(Pause)* You
know, they always say take an aspirin for a headache.
But who wants a headache?

(*Laughs. Sits down on the bed*)

(*Silence*)

(*Laughs, wearily*)

(*Blackout*)

End of Play